Viking History For Kids

A History Series

Children Explore History Book Edition

SPEEDY PUBLISHING

The **Vikings** were a seafaring people from the late eighth to early 11th century who established a name for themselves as traders, explorers and warriors.

They discovered the Americas long before Columbus and could be found as far east as the distant reaches of Russia.

The Viking Age
references
the earliest
recorded
raid in the
790s until
the Norman
Conquest
of England
in 1066.

A Viking raid on the monks of Lindisfarne, a small island located off the northeast coast of England, marked the start of the Viking migration from Scandinavia in 793.

In the years that followed the initial raid, coastal villages, monasteries and even cities found themselves besieged by these sea-based foreign intruders.

The Vikings were famous for sailing huge distances from their home in Scandinavia between AD 800 and 1066 to raid and plunder, but they also traded with people from other countries.

The name
'Viking means
'a pirate raid' in
the Old Norse
language.

Among the many gods Vikings believed in were Thor, the god of thunder, and Loki, a cheeky mischief-maker who could shape-shift to become all different kinds of animals.

The Vikings
were expert
boat builders
and sailors.

The Vikings were eco-pioneers—the 'long houses' where families lived would have turf roofs to help keep in the heat.

When
important
Vikings died,
they would be
placed with all
their clothes,
jewellery, even
their animals,
in a burial ship.

A Viking's most
treasured weapon
was his sword.

Viking longships
could carry at
least sixty men.

Vikings navigated using bearing dials; astronomy; lodestones, sunstones and by releasing captured birds when they thought they were near land.

Vikings believed in two groups of Gods - the Aesir (pronounced "Eye-Ear") and the Vanir.

Vikings loved riddles; sagas; stories and songs.

There were three main classes in Viking society: Jarls (earls) who were noblemen; Karls (average, free Vikings) and Thralls who were slaves.

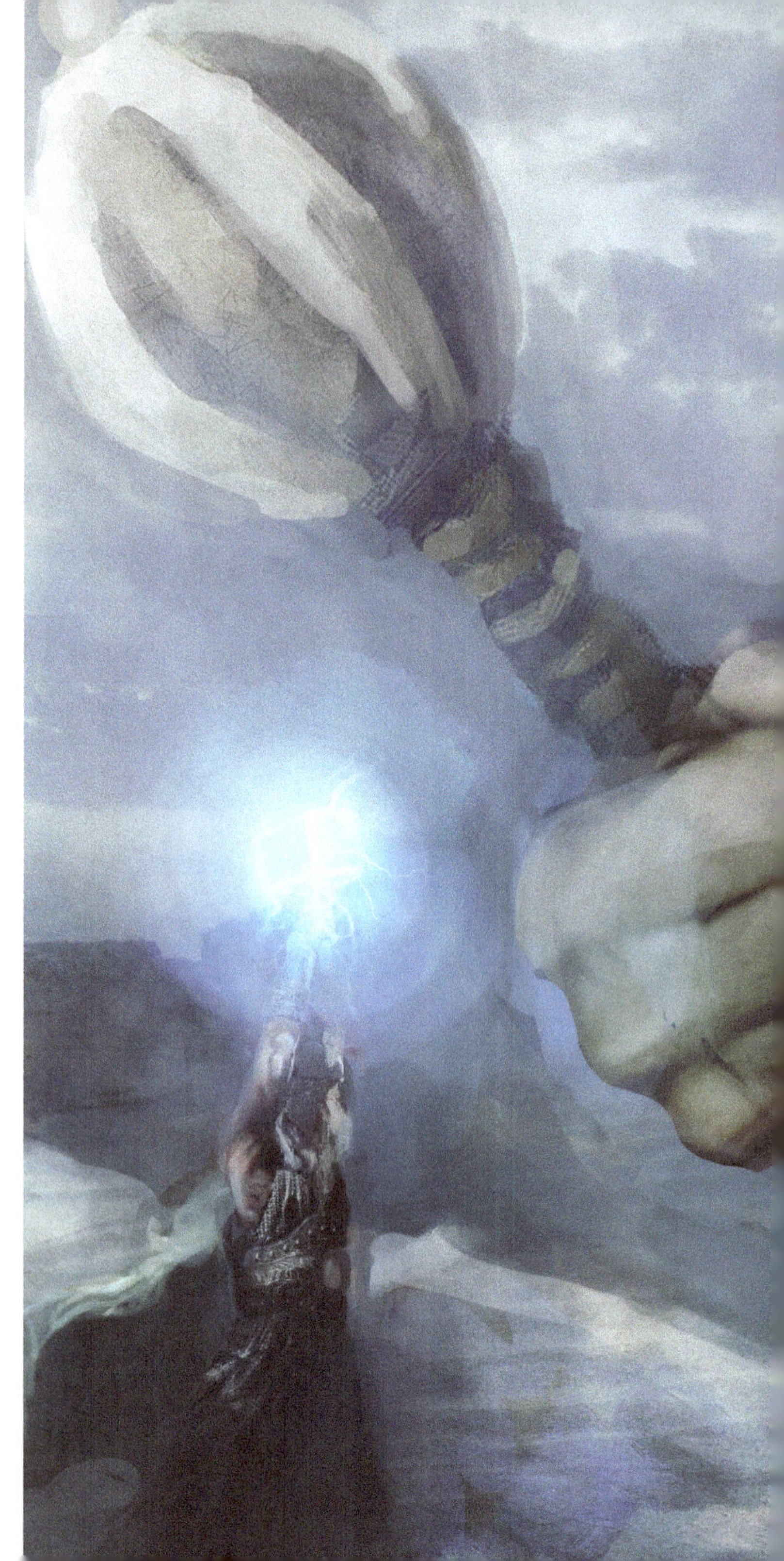

Viking runes were
shaped using
angular strokes
for ease when
carving into wood.

The Viking History is rich and interesting, research and learn more!

Visit
BABY PROFESSOR
EDUCATION KIDS
www.BabyProfessorBooks.com
to download Free Baby Professor eBooks
and view our catalog of new and exciting
Children's Books